**LITTLE
CRAFT BOOK
SERIES**

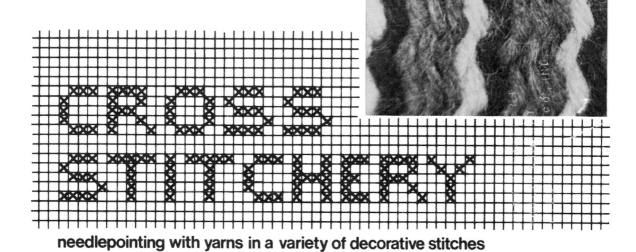

CROSS STITCHERY

needlepointing with yarns in a variety of decorative stitches

By Jo Ippolito Christensen and Sonie Shapiro Ashner

**STERLING
PUBLISHING CO., INC.** NEW YORK
SAUNDERS OF TORONTO, Ltd., Don Mills, Canada

Oak Tree Press Co., Ltd.
London & Sydney

Little Craft Book Series

Dedicated to our parents Lt. Col. and Mrs. Luciano Ippolito and Mrs. Dorothy Shapiro Amdur and in memory of Samuel S. Shapiro.

The authors would like to thank Sonie Ashner's mother and partner in Morningside Knit Shop, Kansas City, Missouri, Mrs. Dorothy Shapiro Amdur, for inspiration.

Thanks to Stuart Ashner, Joy Bauer, Gloria Berenson, Sally Friedman, Sharon Hanlon, Betty Hill and Helen Mickelson for their help in making some of the projects.

Thanks also to Lisa Ashner, Kelly Hanlon, and Carol Whited for posing for pictures.

The authors would like to express their appreciation to artist Luciano Ippolito for the painting on page 36.

Frames on page 36 by Morty Lewkowsky.

Triple Leviathan stitch

Rice stitch

Contents

C804647

Photographs by Marcus Dillon, Jr.
The quotation on the sampler on page 13 was taken from the book entitled *Time Out for Happiness* by Frank B. Gilbreth, Jr., and from a book by his mother, the late Lillian Gilbreth.

Before You Begin

For many centuries needlepoint has been a popular pastime. Women used to sit by the fire stitching useful and decorative items for their homes, incorporating some 200 stitches in their works of art. Today, everyone is re-discovering needlepoint—and those 200 stitches—in bright colors and modern designs.

Needlepoint is embroidery on canvas. Basically, there are three kinds of stitches—horizontal, vertical and diagonal. By combining these component parts, you can create many kinds of stitches. When you place these basic stitches one on top of another, they become *Cross stitches*.

Materials and Methods

There are two kinds of needlepoint canvas—Mono (woven with a single thread) and Penelope (woven with a pair of threads). (See Illus. 1 and 2.) On Mono canvas, one thread is called one mesh, while on Penelope, a pair of threads is called one mesh. Numbers follow the names of the kinds of canvas to indicate the number of mesh per square inch; for example, Penelope 10 and Mono 14. Although *Cross stitches* work up better on Penelope canvas, it is possible to do them on Mono 14. (Directions for this are given on page 21.)

You stitch all needlepoint with a blunt-end tapestry needle, which should be small enough to drop through the holes in the canvas. To thread a needle easily, flatten the yarn between your thumb and index finger. Then push the needle between your fingers and the needle threads itself. Never wet the yarn, as this weakens it. Another way to thread a needle is to cut a rectangle of paper narrow enough to fit the eye of the needle. Fold the paper over the yarn, push it through the eye, and your needle is threaded (see Illus. 3).

As a general rule, use tapestry or Persian yarn in stitching needlepoint pieces. It is moth-proof and it comes in long, strong, fibres. You should not have trouble in matching colors when you run out, for it comes in matched dye lots. It is *essential* that you use either tapestry or Persian yarn for items which will receive lots of wear. Decorative items, on the other hand, may have sections of various yarns for unusual effects (see the doll on page 44). Remember, however, that these yarns do *not* have the strength of tapestry and Persian yarns.

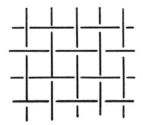

Illus. 1. Mono canvas. One thread is one mesh.

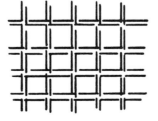

Illus. 2. Penelope canvas. A pair of threads is one mesh.

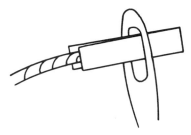

Illus. 3. One method of threading the needle.

Unfortunately, all needlepointers make mistakes every now and then and must rip. To do so, carefully clip the wrong stitches on the right side of the canvas. Turn the canvas over and, using tweezers, pull out the loose threads. Work in any loose ends with a crochet hook. *Never* reuse yarn. The rough canvas wears each strand thin, and re-use just wears it thinner—past the point of beauty. For this reason, you should never stitch with a strand any longer than 18″. If you use weaker, novelty yarns, your strand should be even shorter.

If you inadvertently cut your canvas, simply place another piece of canvas under the hole. Match the holes exactly and baste the new piece in place; then, do needlepoint through both thicknesses.

Spray your finished pieces with a waterproofing product to protect them from dirt. When they need a thorough cleaning, send them to a reputable dry cleaner. Tell him that the fibre content is wool and he will treat your pieces properly.

Purses

Tote Bag

Show off your handiwork in the form of a needlepoint purse or tote bag. The one in Illus. 37 is worked on plastic sheets that resemble Mono canvas and which are available at yarn shops. You need three sheets: one for the front, one for the back, and one for the gussets and the bottom. Cut the third sheet in thirds lengthwise. Plastic sheets are ideal for a tote bag because they have more body than canvas, and, thus, the bag maintains its shape. Also, stitches never distort plastic sheets, as they do canvas. Blocking, then, is not necessary.

It is color, rather than stitches, that gives this purse its stunning design. Using colored pencils or markers, chart any design you wish on graph paper. Be sure the graph paper has the same number of squares per inch as your plastic sheet, which has 10. Otherwise the size of your design will be wrong.

Stitching

Work your design by placing a *Cross stitch* for every square on the graph paper. Begin your first row in the upper left hand corner of the plastic sheet. Start the first stitch just below the second mesh at the top of the sheet. Bring the needle from the wrong side to the right side through the first hole on the left side of the plastic sheet. Pull the yarn through until 1″ remains on the wrong side. As you stitch, work over this end to hold it in place. Next, insert the needle to the wrong side from the right side of

5

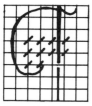

Illus. 4. Half Cross stitch.　　**Illus. 5. Complete the Cross stitch.**

the plastic sheet in the hole diagonally above and to the right of the first one. Come through to the right side in one continuous motion directly under the second hole (Illus. 4). This is called the *Half Cross stitch*.

To complete the rest of the *Cross stitch*, simply reverse the direction of your needle, and work directly over the stitches that you have already worked. This produces a stitch that looks like Illus. 5.

NOTE: You may cross each *Half Cross stitch* as you go if you like (Illus. 6). When you run out of yarn and need to end it, simply run the end under the back of stitches that you have already worked. Never knot the yarn. To begin the next thread, run it under stitches that you have already worked.

Stitch the back and gussets of your purse in the same design. Then use this stitch or another stitch from this book to put your initials on the other side (see page 7).

Assembling

Assemble the purse by stitching the seams with the *Binding stitch*. Line up the holes of the two pieces to be stitched together. Follow Illus. 7 as you read the instructions. Hold the pieces so that the same side is towards you throughout the

stitching of that seam. Call it the front, and the other side the back. Take one stitch in each of the first two holes to secure your stitching. Skip one hole and go into the fourth hole from the back to the front. Go into the second hole from the back; then go into the fifth hole from the back. Then go into the third, sixth, fourth, and so on. Note that you are skipping one space when you move backwards, and that you are going into the next empty space when moving forwards. Always bring the wool over the edge and always go into the back of the canvas. The stitch produces a neat braid. Also work the *Binding stitch* over the top edges to give your purse a finished look.

Attach two sets of chain handles—one end in each corner. Line the purse with sturdy fabric.

Illus. 6. Cross stitch; cross as you go.

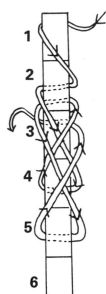

Illus. 7. Use the Binding stitch to sew two pieces together or to neatly finish off an edge.

6

Straw Purse

Decorate a straw bag with needlepoint and ribbon to create a lovely summer purse. Work your initials, name, flowers, or any theme you choose in needlepoint and attach it to the front of the purse.

If you decide to use your initials, sketch them on a piece of graph paper and then "X" in the appropriate squares as shown in Illus. 8.

Measure your purse to see how large a piece of needlepoint it can accommodate. Cut a piece of canvas—Penelope 8 was used for Illus. 38—with the proper dimensions. Add five mesh on each side for a hem. Fold under four of these mesh, leaving one mesh for the edge. Match the holes exactly and baste in place. Do needlepoint through both thicknesses.

The purse in Illus. 38 shows how three different kinds of *Cross stitches* can create an interesting texture. First, work the initials in the *Cross stitch* which is perfectly suited to letters, for it fully fills a square, thus making the letters easier to read. Then work the border in the *Bound Cross stitch* (Illus. 9). This stitch covers a square 4×4 mesh—that is, it covers an area of 4×4 mesh. (Hereafter every cross stitch will be referred to as 2×2, 3×4, 4×4, and so on.) There are three parts to each arm of the cross. It does not matter whether you cross the right arm over the left or the left over the right as long as you do it the same way every time throughout the use of that stitch on any particular piece. (This, by the way, is true for

Illus. 8. Sketch your initials on graph paper and then "X" in the squares.

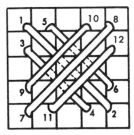

Illus. 9. Bound Cross stitch.

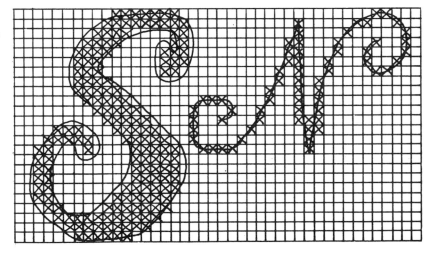

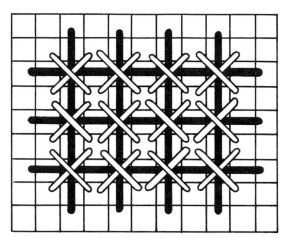

Illus. 10. Double Tramé Cross stitch.

all *Cross stitches*.) As you work, place a small horizontal or vertical stitch between each *Bound Cross stitch* where you have not covered the canvas. Again, it does not matter whether you take a horizontal or vertical stitch, as long as you are consistent.

The background of this purse is done in the *Double Tramé Cross stitch* (see Illus. 10). This stitch is basically a 2 × 2 *Cross stitch*. First fill in the background with the 2 × 2 *Cross stitch*. After you do that, note that the crosses do not completely cover the canvas. At this time, stitch a ground of *Double Tramé*. At the beginning of each row of crosses, bring your needle from the wrong side of the canvas to the right side of the canvas and slip it horizontally under each of the crosses in a horizontal row. Then, at the end of that row, put your needle down into the canvas and come up for the next row. Do not penetrate the canvas in the middle of the row unless you

must stop for the initials. Then, do a vertical row in the same manner. Continue in this way until you have completely covered the background. Work the *Binding stitch* round the edge to give your needlepoint a finished look.

Blocking

Some needlepoint stitches distort your canvas and you must block your piece. Even if the piece is not out of shape, however, you must block it in order to re-set the starch. Insulation board works best for blocking needlepoint because it allows a freer circulation of air, and the needlepoint then dries more quickly. Cover the board with a piece of paper, which you tack or tape in place. This protects your needlepoint from snags and stains. Using a *waterproof* black marker, draw a 1″-grid (criss-crossed, horizontal and vertical lines one inch apart) on the paper. (Do not trust the manufacturer when he says his marker is *waterproof*. Test it yourself.) Dampen your needlepoint piece with cold water; never use hot water, because it shrinks wool. Place your needlepoint on the board. You should block needlepoint that is not textured face *down*, and needlepoint which is textured face *up*. Block this purse face up. Tugging gently, pin one side *in a straight line*, using the grid that you have drawn on the paper as a guide. Push pins or T pins are best to pin with (Illus. 11). Make sure the corner is at a 90-degree angle and then pin the next side in place. Gently, but firmly, pull the other two sides into place, pinning as you go. The pins should be $\frac{1}{2}''$ to $\frac{3}{4}''$ apart so that the tension is even. Do not remove the needlepoint until it is *absolutely dry*, which may take as long as a week.

If your piece is still badly out of shape after blocking, apply rabbit skin glue, which you can buy in art supply shops, to the back.

Finishing

To attach the needlepoint to the straw purse, cover the back of the needlepoint with glue and center it on the purse. Place a weight on top of the needlepoint and allow it to dry for a few minutes only. Thread a needle with yarn the same color as the border. Work it, at a corner, through the purse and the needlepoint and tie it on the wrong side. Do this in each corner and two or three times along each side. Bury the yarn on the right side so that it does not show.

The next step in finishing your purse is to line it. Cut a piece of quilted fabric the length of the inside sides of the purse plus a little extra to fold under, as shown in Illus. 12. Glue the top edge of piece A down. Then wrap the long piece along the inside of the purse. Turn under the raw edge at the end and glue in place. Trace round the bottom of the purse onto a piece of cardboard. Trim the cardboard so that it fits on the inside bottom of the purse. Measure a piece of the lining fabric the same shape as the cardboard bottom pattern, but cut it $1\frac{1}{2}''$ larger on all sides. Glue the fabric to the cardboard, tucking the raw edges around the cardboard. Put a weight on top of this and allow it to dry. Then glue the bottom piece into the bottom of the purse. This completes the inside of your purse.

Weave a wide velvet ribbon through the top of the basket. Make a bow as is shown in Illus. 13.

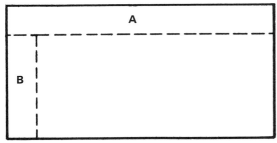

Illus. 12. Cut a piece of fabric for the lining, allowing extra at A and B to turn under.

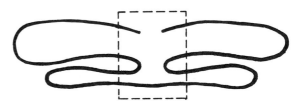

Illus. 13. Make a velvet bow following this pattern. Note that the dotted lines denote a separate piece of velvet.

Suspender Trim

Illus. 39 shows a charming trim for suspenders. First, work out the design completely on graph paper with colored pencils (see Illus. 14). Transfer the design to canvas by working with the *Cross stitch* (see page 6) on Penelope 10 canvas in tapestry or Persian yarn.

When cutting the canvas for your suspender trim, allow a hem of five mesh all the way round, as you did for the straw purse on page 7. Finish the edge with the *Binding stitch* (see page 6).

Block this piece face down as described on page 8.

Attach the suspender trim to leather, fabric, or needlepoint suspenders. Remove the needlepoint for cleaning when necessary.

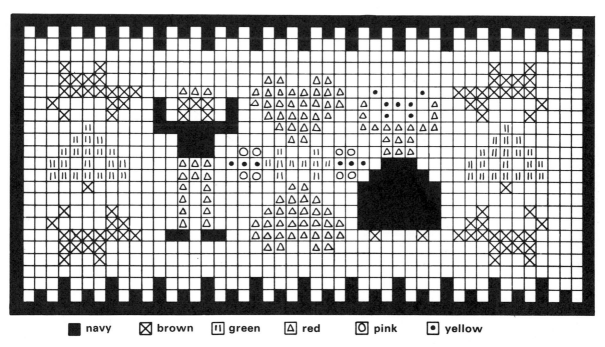

■ navy   ⊠ brown   Ⅲ green   △ red   Ⓞ pink   ● yellow

Illus. 14. Pattern of the design for the suspender trim pictured in color on page 21.

Sewing Box

Decorate a wooden box in which to keep your sewing supplies. Cover the top with needlepoint and make it a pin cushion. The first step is to decide what sort of a design you want on the top of your box. Illus. 18 shows a sewing box with scissors, tape measure, needle, and thread on the top. The tape measure is particularly useful, for it is in full-sized inches. No longer will you have to search far and wide for a tape measure just to measure a few inches.

Sketch each item that you wish to include on paper. Cut them out. (Hint: *trace* around the scissors.) Place the cut-out pieces on another sheet of paper which is exactly the same size as the top of your box. Move them until you are pleased with the composition. When your design is completely finished, re-trace the lines with a black felt-tip marker.

Penelope 8 is a very useful canvas for doing the *Cross stitch*. On the more widely used Penelope 10 canvas, you must split a strand of tapestry yarn to do the *Cross stitch*. Since Penelope 8 is larger, however, you may use a full strand of tapestry yarn to do the *Cross stitch*. Also, since Penelope 8 is larger, your work goes faster. In addition, Penelope 8 is available with a blue thread which counts off every 5 mesh. This is very handy when you have to count mesh for the *Cross stitch*. However, if you are using light-colored yarn, the blue line may show through. It is for this reason that this canvas is *not* recommended for use with light colors.

Whether you choose ecru (beige) or white canvas depends on the colors you intend to use on your needlepoint piece. If you are planning to use white or pastel colors, choose the white canvas; however, if your colors are darker, ecru canvas suits your needs perfectly. Cut your canvas 1″ larger on all sides than the top of your box. Bind the edges with masking tape to prevent ravelling.

To transfer your design onto the canvas, place the canvas on top of your drawing. The black

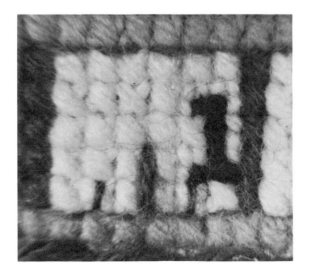

Illus. 15. Close-up of the tape measure on the sewing box pictured on page 13.

11

Illus. 16. Use the Outline stitch to emphasize your design.

lines show through. Trace the design with a grey *waterproof* marker. Grey is best because it does not show through pastel colors and white as black does.

Work the design in *Cross stitch* (Illus. 5). To emphasize your design items (scissors, tape measure, needle and thread), use the *Outline stitch* (Illus. 16). Then, work the background to within $\frac{1}{2}''$ of the edge on all sides. Always personalize your piece by putting your initials and the date in one corner, using the *Cross stitch*. Block your piece.

To attach the needlepoint to the top of the box, fold under the raw edge of the canvas and tack it to the edge of the box along one side with *small* nails or a staple gun. Tack down two more sides. There should be extra fullness since the needlepoint is larger than the top of the box. Stuff the area between the needlepoint and the top of the box with steel wool, which keeps your pins and needles sharp. Tack the fourth side in place. Crochet a chain of matching or contrasting yarn, or buy an attractive trim to use. Place it, wrong side up, along the edge of the canvas. Glue it in place to cover the nails or staples. Pile in your sewing supplies and admire your practical handiwork.

Illus. 17 (right). Mosaic stitch.

Sampler

If there is a particular quotation or motto you like, put it in needlepoint. If you do not have a special one, perhaps the one in Illus. 19 will strike your fancy. Chart the letters and their placement on graph paper. Work the letters in the *Cross stitch*.

Penelope 8, as has been mentioned on page 11, is very useful for the *Cross stitch*. Notice in Illus. 19, however, that you can see dark vertical lines in the yellow portion. These lines are where the blue thread was. The blue thread showed through the yellow, so the authors pulled the blue thread out, but it left a space and it still shows. Keep this problem in mind when you choose yarn colors to work on Penelope 8 that has this blue thread.

The background of this sampler is worked in a stitch, which, although it resembles a *Cross stitch*, is actually not. It is called the *Mosaic stitch* (see Illus. 17). This is a set of three diagonal stitches: short, long, short. Each set covers a 2 × 2 square. It is much faster to work than a 2 × 2 cross. Refer back to page 8; note that when you did a 2 × 2 cross on Penelope 8, it was necessary to

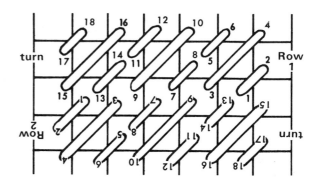

Illus. 18. A sewing box cover which includes an actual-sized tape measure is a practical as well as decorative use for your needlepoint.

Illus. 19. How true this is! If you cannot think of another saying or motto that you like, why not chart this one on graph paper and then on your canvas?

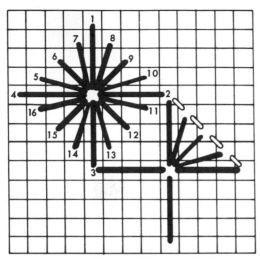

Illus. 20. Diamond Eyelet stitch.

Illus. 21. Close-up of the Mosaic stitch and the Diamond Eyelet stitch in the sampler.

round the letters in *Cross stitch*.and pick up the *Mosaic stitch* just outside the lettering.

Since pearls are mentioned in the quote on the sampler, it seems appropriate to include them in the border, which is worked in the *Diamond Eyelet stitch* (see Illus. 20). This stitch covers a diamond-shaped area on 8×8 mesh and is made up of 16 completely separate stitches, each of which go *into* the center. It is easier to make the four longest stitches that form the upright cross first. Each of these stitches is over four mesh.

Since the *Diamond Eyelet* does not cover the canvas completely between each of the diamond-shaped areas, you must use an *Outline stitch* (see Illus. 16). Sew a pearl in the center of each of the *Diamond Eyelets*, using regular sewing thread and a needle small enough to go through the hole in the pearl. Block face up.

Cut a piece of Masonite (pressed board) or canvas board $\frac{1}{4}''$ smaller on all sides than your finished needlepoint. Center the needlepoint over the board and fold the margin of canvas to the back side. With carpet thread, lace the sides and the top and bottom together. Insert the mounted needlepoint into a ready-made frame. (In order for your sampler to fit into a ready-made frame, you must plan ahead. Otherwise, you will have to have a frame made to fit.) Obtain a piece of brown paper which is at least one inch bigger than the back side of the frame. Dampen it with a sponge. Apply glue to the back of the frame. Turn the frame onto the paper. Place weights on top of the frame—not on top of the needlepoint. When the glue and the paper are dry, trim away the excess paper with a single-edged razor blade or artist's knife. Your sampler is ready to hang.

lay a *Double Tramé* to cover the canvas. The *Mosaic stitch* covers the canvas in the same 2×2 square with much less work. It is not even necessary to figure out the *Mosaic* behind the letters. Therefore, you can do the area right

Covers and Cases

Telephone Book Cover

Make a permanent cover for your telephone book. Illus. 26 gives you one idea to follow. Enlarge a drawing of a phone by using the grid method. Draw a $\frac{1}{4}''$-grid—criss-crossed lines $\frac{1}{4}''$ apart—over the picture to be enlarged. On another sheet of paper, draw a $1''$-grid—criss-crossed lines $1''$ apart—with the same number of squares. Copy the portions of the drawing in each of the small squares into the corresponding large squares. These dimensions increase the size of your original drawing four times. By changing the size of both grids, you can change the size of the final design. Once the drawing is the proper size, trace it onto the canvas.

Penelope 10 canvas has been used here to achieve more detail. Also, smaller canvas produces greater wearability. Cut your canvas so that it is as long as the phone book cover is high. Add five mesh to compensate for shrinkage, and five mesh to the top and to the bottom for hems (you should have 15 mesh over and above the height of the phone book). The width of the canvas should be the length of the phone book—the front, back, and spine, plus 6'' on each end for flaps—measured with a tape measure while the telephone book is closed. Fold under the top and bottom hems four mesh, leaving one mesh for the edge as you did on page 7. Work the background through both thicknesses of canvas.

The telephone and telephone numbers here are stitched in the 2 × 2 *Cross stitch*, which does cover Penelope 10. The push buttons on the

Illus. 22. Close-up of the push buttons (Smyrna Cross stitch) on the telephone.

phone are the *Smyrna Cross stitch* (see Illus. 23), which adds a great deal of texture. A hint in making the *Smyrna Cross* is to work the X (numbered 1 to 4 in Illus. 23) first. The background is the *Mosaic stitch* (see Illus. 17).

If you have children, you may wish to personalize your phone book cover by adding outlines of their hands (or anyone else's, of course) on the back cover. Trace round the hands and transfer the design to canvas. Work the names and the inside of the hands in the 2 × 2 *Cross*

Illus. 23. Smyrna Cross stitch.

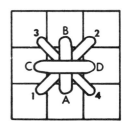

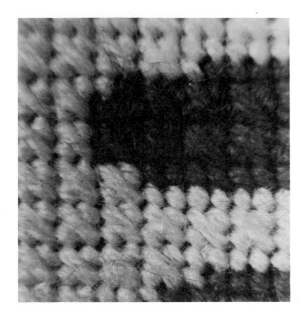

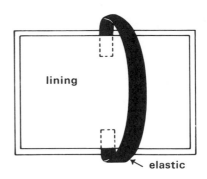

Illus. 24. For a small phone book, glue cardboard to the back of the needlepoint and cover the cardboard with lining. Insert elastic as shown, between the cardboard and the lining.

Illus. 25 (left). Close-up of the dark blue finger (Cross stitch) in Illus. 26. Note the Mosaic. stitch background.

stitch. Since the *Smyrna Cross* creates texture, block your piece face up.

After your needlepoint has dried, place the cover on your phone book and tuck the flaps around the outside cover. Close the book. Remove the needlepoint cover from the book, marking the fold line for the flaps with pins or basting thread. Use the *Binding stitch* to sew the flaps to the cover at the top and bottom of the cover. Continue working the *Binding stitch* round the top and bottom of the cover, even though you are not sewing a seam. This gives a finished look. Slip the cover on to the phone book. If your phone book does not have a hard cover, glue stiff cardboard to its front and back covers before putting the needlepoint cover on.

If you have a very small phone book, or if you wish to cover a television program guide, do not make flaps on the cover. Stop stitching at the fold line for the flaps. Turn under the hem as you did on the top and bottom. Work the *Binding stitch* on the edges. Because the wrong side of your needlepoint will show, line the inside of the cover. To do this, first glue two pieces of stiff cardboard to the wrong side of the needlepoint. Be sure the break in the two pieces of cardboard corresponds to the center spine so that the cover will bend. Glue felt or hand stitch another lining fabric over the cardboard. Attach a piece of elastic to the center with the ends between the cardboard and the lining, as shown in Illus. 24. Slip the phone book between the elastic and the cover.

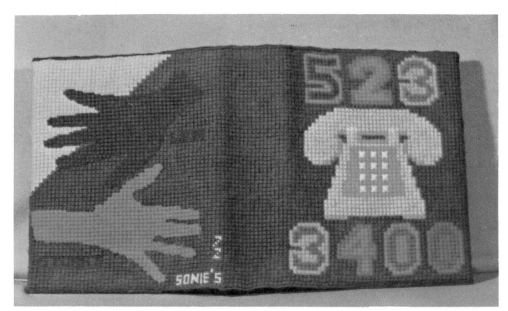

Illus. 26 (above). Make a hand-some cover for your phone book which serves the dual purpose of protecting the book.

Illus. 27 (right). Even if you are not a champion tennis player, you will be the talk of the courts with this racket cover.

Tennis Racket Cover

Cover your tennis racket with needlepoint as shown in Illus. 27 and on the back cover. Trace round your tennis racket on a sheet of paper, adding 1″ all the way round for ease. Transfer your design onto Penelope 8 canvas. Turn under a four-mesh hem, with one mesh for the edge, at the narrow neck of the handle only. Do *not* turn under the canvas anywhere else.

17

The turtle's body is worked in the *Double Straight Cross stitch* (see Illus. 28), which is composed of a 2 × 2 diagonal cross superimposed on a 4 × 4 *Upright Cross*, which you make from two perpendicular stitches (see Illus. 29). Do the *Upright Cross* first. The head is the *Italian Cross stitch* (see Illus. 31), which is a 2 × 2 *Cross stitch* with an *Outline stitch* worked on alternate rows. The feet, neck, and tail are worked in the *Double stitch* (see Illus. 32), a combination of a 3 × 1 *Oblong Cross stitch* and a 1 × 1 *Cross stitch*. The grass is in the *Chain stitch* (see Illus. 33), which is very readily adaptable to curves. The background is worked in the *Alternating Oblong Cross* (see Illus. 35). Work the background through both thicknesses where you have folded under the hem. Block face up.

To make the back, use the same pattern as you did for the needlepoint. Cut the back of your cover from vinyl or any sturdy fabric. Do not

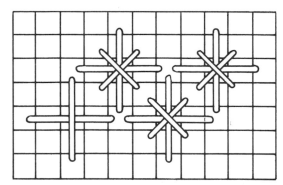

Illus. 28. Double Straight Cross stitch.

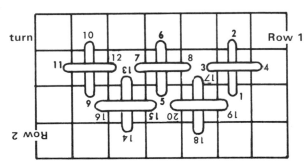

Illus. 29. Upright Cross stitch.

Illus. 30. Close-up of the Italian Cross stitch.

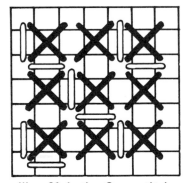

Illus. 31. Italian Cross stitch.

18

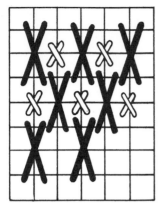

Illus. 32. Double stitch.

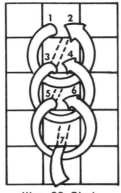

Illus. 33. Chain stitch.

forget to add $\frac{5}{8}$″-seam allowances all the way round except at the bottom where the handle is; add 2″ there (see Illus. 36). Turn up the 2″-hem and stitch by hand. Place the right sides of the needlepoint and the fabric backing together. Be sure you have placed them correctly before you stitch them together. Insert a 9″ neck-type zipper in the side seam. Follow the directions on the zipper package to sew in the zipper. Then stitch the side seams by machine.

Trim the canvas even with the fabric. Zig-zag, or over-cast by hand, the two seam allowances. Turn and insert your tennis racket.

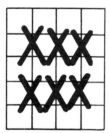

Illus. 34. Oblong Cross stitch.

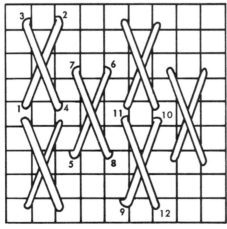

Illus. 35. Alternating Oblong Cross stitch.

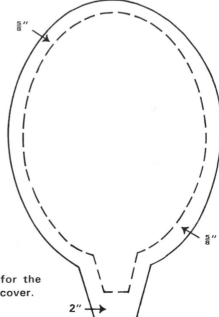

Illus. 36. Cutting pattern for the back of the tennis racket cover.

19

Illus. 38. The size of the straw purse you choose determines, of course, how large your original needlepoint adornment should be.

Illus. 37. You can stitch an elegant purse like this one simply using the Cross stitch, or you can choose any other of the decorative stitches explained in this book.

Illus. 39. Copy this little picture to trim a child's suspenders, or create an original design instead.

Illus. 40. You will pat yourself proudly on the back if you buy a large, uncovered button and cover it with needlepoint. Cut Mono 14 canvas according to the pattern accompanying the uncovered button and then plot and stitch—with one strand of Persian yarn—a Cross stitch design to adorn a bought or hand-made dress. (For Mono canvas, you must cross each stitch as you go.) Also try using Penelope 10 and stitch with tapestry yarn and embroidery floss.

Key Case

This key case is just the perfect thing as a gift item. It is also good for yourself for that quick trip to the grocery store, for inside the key case is a place for your driver's licence and your money.

Illus. 49 and 50 show ideas for decorating the front and back of a key case, which is actually two pieces of canvas—even just scraps—which you sew together with the *Binding stitch* (see page 6) on three sides. Cut two pieces of canvas 4″ × 5″. This includes five mesh on all sides for hems. Turn them under as you have before—four mesh for the hem and one for the edge. Cut the canvas if necessary. Put your initials on one side and add snowflakes—placed at random—for winter. The following stitches suggest snowflakes:

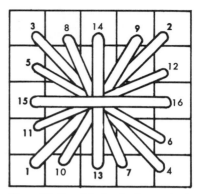

Illus. 42. Double Leviathan stitch.

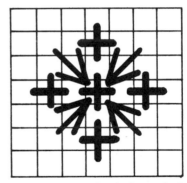

Illus. 43. Triple Leviathan stitch.

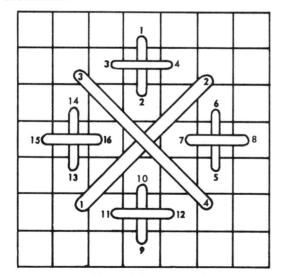

Illus. 41. Double Cross stitch.

Diamond Eyelet (see Illus. 20 page 14).

Double Cross (see Illus. 41), for which you use a double strand of tapestry yarn to work a 4 × 4 *Cross stitch* on both sides. At the top and bottom, add an *Upright Cross*.

Double Leviathan (see Illus. 42), made up of eight stitches which cover a 4 × 4 square. Do the X first and do the *Upright Cross* last.

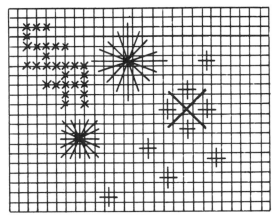

Illus. 44. Pattern for the winter side of the key case. Stitches that resemble snowflakes are: Diamond Eyelet stitch, Double Cross stitch, Double Leviathan stitch, Triple Leviathan stitch, and Upright Cross stitch.

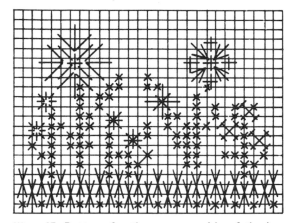

Illus. 45. Pattern for the summer side of the case. Stitches are:
Grass: Alternating Oblong Cross stitch
Leaves and background: Cross stitch
Flowers: Double Straight Cross stitch, Medallion stitch, Rice stitch, Smyrna Cross stitch, Star stitch

Triple Leviathan (see Illus. 43), which covers a square 6 × 6 mesh. The *Upright Crosses* are 2 × 2 and they touch.

Upright Cross, which is two mesh high and two mesh wide (see page 18).

Flowers are suggested by the following stitches: *Double Straight Cross stitch* (see page 18).

Medallion stitch, best done by following Illus.

Illus. 46. Medallion stitch.

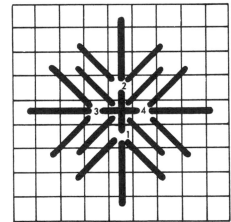

Illus. 47. Rice stitch.

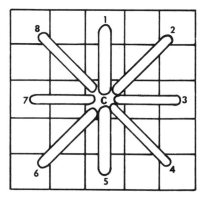

Illus. 48. Star stitch.

46. Hint: make the small *Upright Cross* in the center last. This stitch covers a square 8 × 8 mesh.

Rice stitch (see Illus. 47), a 2 × 2 *Cross* with each of its arms tied down by a 1 × 1 *Half Cross* which slants in the opposite direction from the arm which it ties down.

Smyrna Cross (see page 15).

Star stitch (see Illus. 48), which covers a 4 × 4 square made up of eight stitches, all going *into* the center of the star. It is easier to work if you do the four stitches that form the *Upright Cross* first.

Work the grass in the *Alternating Oblong Cross* (see Illus. 35). Work the leaves and the background in the *Cross stitch*. See Illus. 44 and 45 for a pattern key for both sides of the key case.

Block each of the pieces. When dry, sew three sides together with the *Binding stitch*. Go across the tops of both fourth sides separately with the *Binding stitch* to give a finished look. When going round the corners, treat each corner as if it were two holes. Attach the key ring to one corner with the *Binding stitch*.

If you wish to line your key case, use a long-wearing fabric of a matching or contrasting color. Make it ¼″ smaller on all sides than the needlepoint. Stitch three sides together. Insert it into the key chain with the wrong sides together. Turn under the raw edge at the top and hand stitch in place. Hand sew velcro—a material which sticks to itself and is, therefore, often used in closings—across the top for a closing. Put the velcro as close to one corner as you can get it. Leave room for your finger to get in at the other corner, otherwise you will not be able to open the case very easily.

Illus. 49 (above). Even the personalized initials on this side of the key case fit into this crisp, winter scene.

Illus. 50 (left). For the other side, reproduce this colorful scene or stitch any original summer décor that you like.

Home Aids

Table-Top Catch-All

People who do any sort of hand work are con-continually plagued by piles of yarn, scraps and other trash. If you have this problem, decorate an attractive table-top catch-all for these things. Illus. 54 gives a colorful suggestion on how to cover a tin coffee can to serve this useful purpose.

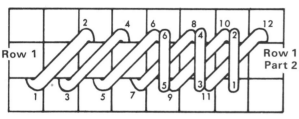

Illus. 51. Slanting Cross stitch.

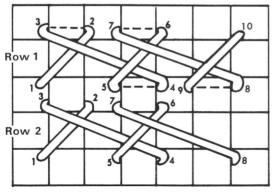

Illus. 52. Greek stitch.

Cut Penelope 8 canvas so that it is as long as a one-pound tin coffee can is high plus two extra mesh in length to allow for the thickness of the plastic lid which you place on the bottom of the can to protect your table from scratches. Also add five mesh at the top and again at the bottom for hems. Measure the circumference of the coffee container. Make your canvas that wide—plus an extra 6″ to account for the bulk of the yarn and the seam allowance.

Draw an area on a sheet of paper which corresponds to the size canvas that you need to cover the coffee container. It is within this area that you must draw your design. Use the one pictured in Illus. 54 as a guide or design one of your own. Transfer it to the canvas as described on page 11.

Prepare your canvas for stitching by turning under four mesh for a hem and one mesh for the edge at the top and bottom. Do *not* turn under any edges on the ends of the canvas. Begin stitching. See Illus. 53 for a complete key to the stitches in Illus. 54. Some of the stitches that you have already learned are most appropriate for flowers and mushrooms—the *Cross stitch* (see Illus. 5), *Double Cross stitch* (see Illus. 41), *Medallion stitch* (see Illus. 46), *Smyrna Cross stitch* (see Illus. 23), and *Triple Leviathan stitch* (see Illus. 43).

In addition, the *Slanting Cross stitch* makes a most effective and interesting pattern (see Illus. 51). It is a 2 × 2 cross in which the bottom arm of the cross is a diagonal stitch and the top arm is a straight stitch.

The *Greek stitch* is another *Cross stitch* with arms of unequal length (see Illus. 52). Actually, it

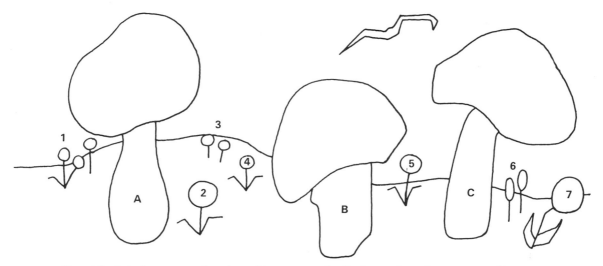

Illus. 53. Stitch pattern for the table-top catch-all shown in color on page 28:
Mushrooms

Caps		Stems	
A	Double Cross stitch		Smyrna Cross stitch
B	Slanting Cross stitch		Fern stitch
C	Greek stitch		Spaced Cross Tramé (1 x 1)

Flowers
1, 3, 6 : Cross stitch   Sky : Flying Cross stitch
2 : Triple Leviathan stitch   Grass : Spaced Cross Tramé (1 x 3)
4, 5 : Smyrna Cross stitch   Stems and leaves : Cross stitch
7 : Medallion stitch   Bird : Cross stitch

Initials and date : Cross stitch

has one short arm and one long arm. Each *Greek stitch* is intertwined with the next one, and you must work it *only* from the left to the right, using a double strand of tapestry yarn. The short

arm is a 2 × 2 diagonal upwards and to the right. Next, bring the needle up in the same row, two mesh to the left. Make a 4 × 2 diagonal downwards and to the right. Bring up the needle two mesh to the left in the same row. Repeat these moves to the end of the row. To start the second row, come back to the beginning of the first row and start directly below it.

The *Fern stitch* is a stitch which takes its form in vertical rows (see Illus. 55). You must work it only from top to bottom. Take a 2 × 2 diagonal stitch downwards and to the right. Bring the needle up one mesh to the left in the same row. Take a 2 × 2 diagonal stitch upwards and to the right. Begin the second stitch one mesh below the hole where you began the first stitch. To

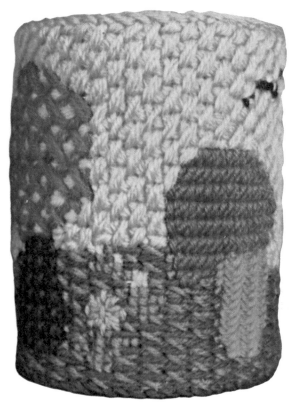

Illus. 54. If you always wonder what to do with empty tin coffee cans, why not be practical as well as creative and make a decorative table-top catch-all?

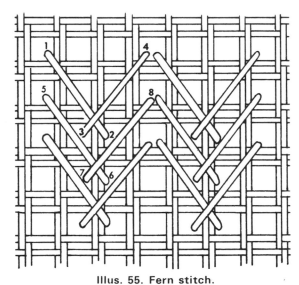

Illus. 55. Fern stitch.

28

begin a new vertical column, go back up to the top and work down again.

The *Flying Cross stitch* gives a look of diagonal line which swirls round the coffee container. It is a 3 × 2 cross, worked with double yarn. The second cross starts one mesh directly below the first one (see Illus. 58). Do not confuse this stitch with the *Alternating Oblong Cross stitch* (Illus. 35).

The *Spaced Cross Tramé* (Illus. 57) can give different looks according to how you work it. For example, mushroom stem C is worked in a 1 × 1 *Cross stitch* arranged in a checkerboard pattern. A vertical *Tramé* is then run from under one cross to the next as was done on page 8. The grass, also worked in *Spaced Cross Tramé*, looks completely different. The crosses are also laid in a checkerboard pattern, but they are 1 × 3 (Illus. 59) and the *Tramé* is horizontal. This makes a great deal of difference in how the stitch looks. In addition, the grass was done in two shades of green, with the darker color the *Tramé*.

Illus. 56. Close-ups of the Greek stitch (top) and the Alternating Oblong Cross stitch (bottom).

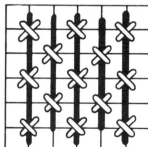

Illus. 57. Spaced Cross Tramé (1 x 1).

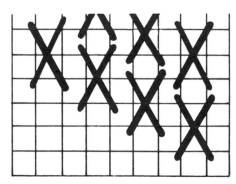

Illus. 58. Flying Cross stitch.

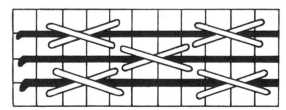

Illus. 59. Spaced Cross Tramé (1 x 3).

Work the design to within 1″ of the circumference of the coffee container. For example, if the container is 10″ in circumference, work just 9″.

Next, block your needlepoint face up (see Illus. 60). After it has dried, wrap it round the coffee container until it fits snugly. Loosen it one mesh and pin. With a waterproof felt-tip marker, mark the place on both ends where the seam will be. (This extra mesh is to make it easy for the needlepoint to go over the plastic lid.) Then remove the needlepoint piece from the tin can. Trim the excess canvas to within 1″ of the marks on each end. Overlap the marks on each end of the canvas. Baste in place. Continue your design and the background across the seam, working the needlepoint through both thicknesses. Let the design meet at the mark.

Work the *Binding stitch* round the top of the tin can in a yarn the same color as the sky. Then work the *Binding stitch* round the bottom of the can in a yarn the same color as the grass. You have now completed your needlepoint.

You should be able to slip the needlepoint over the tin can and over the lid at the bottom without any difficulty. Also, you should not need any glue to secure it.

Illus. 60. After you finish your needlepoint, make a blocking board as described on page 8, dampen your creation, and carefully pin it in place with T pins or push pins, as shown here. Blocking restores shape and also re-sets the starch in the canvas.

Owl Apron-Tote Bag

Carry the handy apron-tote bag in Illus. 66 with you to meetings or to a friend's for coffee. The top part of the apron tucks into the owl pocket and keeps your handiwork dust-free and also acts as an aid in keeping your things inside. When you arrive, put the apron on and all the materials that you need to knit, crochet or needlepoint are at your fingertips. Wear the apron at home, also, while you are working. When the telephone rings, your things will not slip to the floor when you get up to answer it. The apron also keeps lint and yarn off your clothes. You carry it by two nylon cord handles you attach to the inside of the pocket and to the wrong side of the apron.

Cut Penelope 8 canvas 17″ wide and 12″ high. Sketch your design and trace it onto the canvas as described on page 11. Bind the edges with masking tape to prevent ravelling. As you work your needlepoint, leave a 1″-margin of blank canvas all the way round.

Various stitches were used in making the owls (see Illus. 67). Those that you already know include the 2 × 2 *Cross stitch*, *Double stitch*, *Greek stitch*, 3 × 1 *Oblong Cross stitch*, the *Rice stitch* and *Upright Cross stitch*.

New stitches include:

Buttonhole stitch (see Illus. 62). Bring the needle out of the canvas at 1. Insert the needle at 2 and bring it out at 3, on top of the yarn loop. Continue as in Illus. 62. Practice on a scrap before you put this stitch on your canvas.

Combination Cross stitch (see Illus. 63). Work 2 × 2 *Cross stitches* first. Fill in the spaces with 2 × 2 *Upright Crosses*.

Illus. 61. Here, the versatile apron-tote bag is an apron.

Illus. 62. Buttonhole stitch.

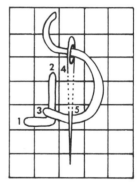

Illus. 63 (below). Combination Cross stitch.

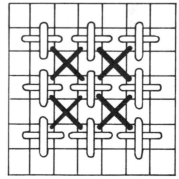

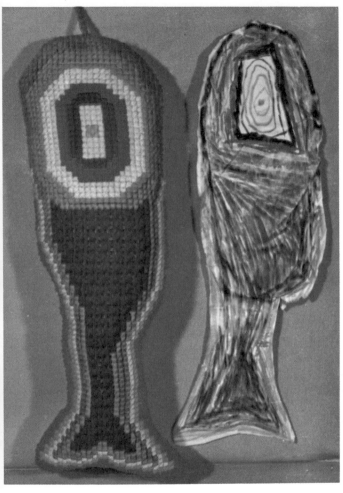

Illus. 64. Use a child's artwork as inspiration for your own or the child's needlepoint! This carp was actually stitched on Penelope 4, a large canvas, by a young boy. Trace the drawing onto the canvas, leaving a 2- to 3-inch margin all the way round, stitch in the Cross stitch, and then complete as instructed for the doll on page 46. For a fishing line as shown, simply crochet a chain of yarn and attach it to the fish's mouth.

Illus. 65. Practice the various Cross stitches you like on one piece of canvas and the result should be as unique as this multi-stitch pillow. See page 43 for this pillow's stitch pattern.

Illus. 66. What a handy household item this is! Here, this attractively stitched apron-tote is being carried as a tote bag.

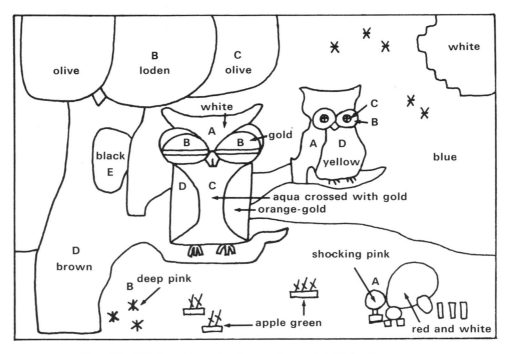

Illus. 67. Stitch pattern for the owl apron-tote bag:

Tree: A, B, C: Turkey Work
       D: Greek stitch, worked so it slants upwards
       E: Knotted stitch

Big Owl: A: Continental stitch
         B: Crossed Filling stitch
         C: Rice stitch
         D: Crossed Cashmere stitch, in reverse directions

Small Owl: A: Hitched Cross stitch
           B: Buttonhole stitch
           C: Upright Cross stitch
           D: Turkey Work

Sky: Oblong Cross stitch
Mushroom: Combination Cross stitch
Grass: Double stitch
Tufts: Knotted stitch
Flowers: A: Rococo stitch   Stars: Hitched Cross stitch
         B: Slashed Cross stitch   Cloud: Cross stitch

Crossed Cashmere stitch (see Illus. 68). This is a set of four diagonal stitches covering a rectangle 3 × 2. Work from right to left *or* from top to bottom. The short stitches are 1 × 1 and the long stitches are 2 × 2. Cross the long stitches with a straight stitch, one mesh tall. Reverse the direction of the stitch for the right and left wings of the owl.

Crossed Filling stitch. See Illus. 69 and 71.

Hitched Cross stitch (see Illus. 70 and 72). This is a 3 × 2 cross with a 1 × 2 diagonal tie.

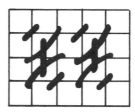

Illus. 68. Crossed Cashmere stitch.

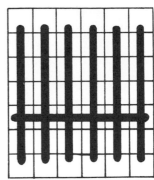

Illus. 69 (right). Crossed Filling stitch.

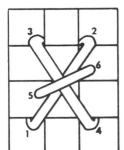

Illus. 70. Hitched Cross stitch.

Illus. 71. Close-up of the big owl's eye (Crossed Filling stitch).

Illus. 72. Close-up of the stars (Hitched Cross stitch) in the sky (Oblong Cross stitch).

C804647

35

Illus. 73 (left). If you do not know an artist, or do not have an original painting such as this one, you could also trace or enlarge (using the grid method described on page 15) any other reproduction you admire.

Illus. 74 (right). If it is possible to enhance the beauty of an original painting, needlepoint may be the way to do it! Notice how effectively the simple, elegant lines of the painting have been transformed into breath-taking Cross stitchery.

Knotted stitch (see Illus. 75 and 78), in which each slanted stitch is 3 × 1 and is tied in the middle with a *Reverse Half Cross stitch.* Work the second row by going into the previous row.

Rococo stitch (see Illus. 76). This covers a square 4 × 4 mesh. Work four vertical stitches between two vertical mesh and over four mesh in height. Tie each vertical stitch down, as shown in Illus. 76, *as you make it.* Do *not* put in all four stitches and then tie them down.

Slashed Cross stitch (see Illus. 77). This is a 4 × 4 *Upright Cross* with a 2 × 2 diagonal tie.

Turkey Work (see Illus. 79). Work this stitch only from *left* to *right* and from *bottom* to *top.* Start your yarn on the *right* side of the canvas at 1. Come out at 2. Go in again at 3 and out at 4.

Illus. 76. Rococo stitch.

Illus. 77. Slashed Cross stitch.

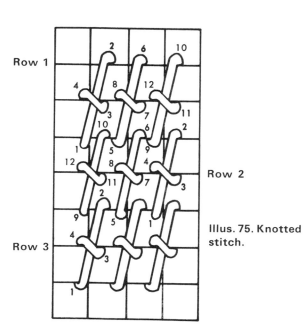

Illus. 75. Knotted stitch.

Row 1

Row 2

Row 3

Illus. 78. Close-up of a tuft (Knotted stitch) in the grass (Double stitch) of the apron-tote bag.

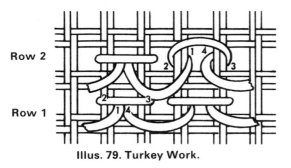

Row 2

Row 1

Illus. 79. Turkey Work.

Place the next stitch in the next hole. Pull the second stitch tightly, and every other one thereafter. Loop the yarn downwards after you pull the stitch tightly. Loop it upwards for the next stitch. Loops may be of variable length, cut or uncut.

Work with a double strand of tapestry yarn throughout the whole piece except for the sky, grass, large mushroom cap and baby owl's stomach. Block your needlepoint piece face up.

Choose a piece of solid color, permanent press fabric for your apron. Cut a piece $19\frac{1}{2}'' \times 39''$ for the apron; cut a piece $3\frac{1}{2}'' \times 13\frac{1}{2}''$ for the waistband. Turn under the raw edges (see Illus. 80, line A) $\frac{1}{4}''$ along the long sides and press. Then fold the same edges under 1″ (line B). Press. Turn under one of the short sides $\frac{1}{4}''$ (line C) and press. Then turn the same side under one inch (line D). Press.

Illus. 80. Cut a piece of an attractive, solid color, permanent press fabric for the apron, following these dimensions.

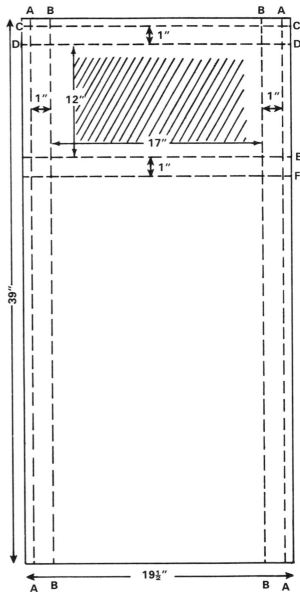

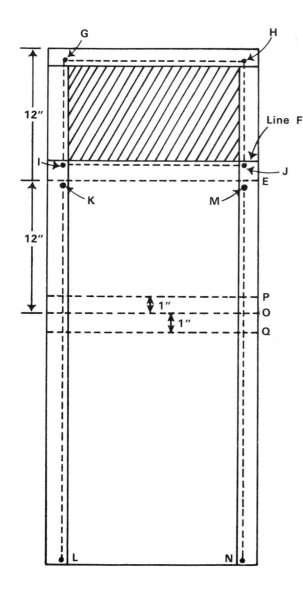

Remove the tape from the needlepoint. Lay the needlepoint into the folds with the top edge of needlepoint under lines C and D. Pin in place. Fold the bottom piece of fabric onto the top of the needlepoint on line E. Fold the top piece of fabric down on line F. Press. Pin in place. Your piece should now look like Illus. 81.

Stitch on the machine from point G to point H along the dotted line; then stitch from point I to point J, from K to L and from M to N along the dotted line. Fold the bottom piece of fabric under on line O. Lines P and Q fall on top of each other. Stitch on line P–Q. Press the tuck down. Fold the bottom piece of fabric under on line E. Press. Pin together.

Stitch from G to I and from H to J along the dotted lines. Gather the top edge of the apron (where points L and N are) to fit a $13\frac{1}{2}$" waistband. Attach a piece of grosgrain ribbon to the ends of the waistband for apron ties. Tack a piece of nylon cord along the inside edge of the pocket and on the inside of the tuck on the wrong side of the apron. Burn the ends of the cord (the nylon melts) to keep it from fraying.

If you do not want an apron, you can, of course, simply frame your needlepoint.

Illus. 81. After you have made the proper folds and have placed your needlepoint into position, your piece should look like this.

Pillows

Multi-Stitch Pillow

Make a pillow, the most popular item made from needlepoint, to show off your ability to make decorative needlepoint cross stitches. Because a pillow is an item which does not receive lots of wear, you may use your yarn scraps to create textures. The heather tones, which are not available in tapestry yarn, make unusually interesting patterns. The pillow in Illus. 65 is made from wool sport yarn which is equivalent to two plies of a three-ply Persian strand. In most cases, this weight yarn covers the Mono 14 canvas that was used for this project. The larger cross stitches require a double strand.

This Mono 14 canvas is a new Mono canvas made from a pair of interlocking threads which stabilizes the horizontal and vertical threads at each junction (see Illus. 82). Thus, restrictions for working certain stitches on Mono canvas no longer apply.

The stitches in this pillow that you already know are: *Continental stitch, Cross stitch, Diamond Eyelet stitch, Double stitch, Greek Cross stitch, Mosaic stitch, Rice stitch, Triple Leviathan stitch,* and *Upright Cross stitch.*

New stitches include:

Straight Gobelin stitch (see Illus. 84). This is a vertical stitch over two mesh. Use it to separate the squares of stitches.

Patterned Crosses with *Scotch stitch.* Work a checkerboard pattern of three components: *Smyrna Cross stitch, Scotch stitch* (see Illus. 83), and *Straight Gobelin stitch.* In Row 1, work one *Scotch stitch,* one block of five *Straight Gobelin stitches* (over four mesh), one *Scotch stitch,* one block of

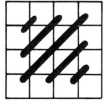

Illus. 82. New Mono canvas with interlocking threads.

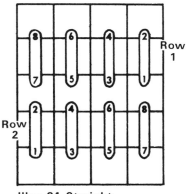

Illus. 84. Straight Gobelin stitch.

Illus. 83. Scotch stitch.

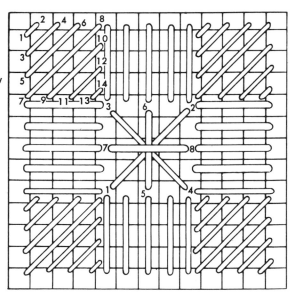

Illus. 85. Patterned Crosses with Scotch stitch.

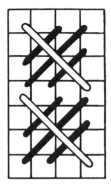

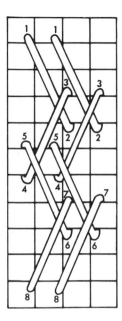

Illus. 86. Crossed Scotch stitch.

Illus. 87. Plaited Gobelin stitch.

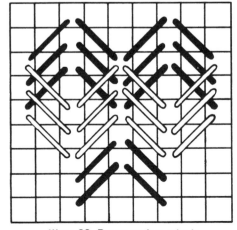

Illus. 88. Perspective stitch.

vertical *Straight Gobelin stitches*, and so on. Compose Row 2 of one block of horizontal *Straight Gobelin stitches*, one *Smyrna Cross*, one block of horizontal *Straight Gobelin stitches*, one *Smyrna Cross*, and so on. Repeat Rows 1 and 2 until you have covered the area to be worked (see Illus. 85 for the pattern.)

Plaited Gobelin stitch (see Illus. 87). For this, you must work this stitch in vertical rows. To begin another row, go back to the top and work downwards again.

Crossed Scotch stitch. This stitch is very similar to the *Scotch stitch* in Illus. 83. Compare Illus. 83 and 86 and note that the two smallest stitches have been omitted and that a diagonal stitch crosses the three center stitches. Use a second color for the cross stitch.

Perspective stitch (see Illus. 88). This stitch, not effective in one color, is reminiscent of a perspective view of a box. The st tch consists of three pairs of 2 × 2 stitches superimposed in an inverted position on three pairs of stitches of the same size. First make a 2 × 2 diagonal stitch upwards and to the right. Place two more identical stitches below the first. From the holes where the first three stitches end, begin three more diagonal stitches—this time downwards and to the right. You now have a three-stripe chevron pointing up. With a second color, super-impose another three-stripe chevron, this time pointing down. Begin the second set of stitches so that the top of the first stitch of the second set and the bottom of the first stitch of the first set share the same hole. The second row fits between the first.

Leaf stitch (see Illus. 89). This stitch consists of

41

a set of five pairs of stitches plus a vertical stitch. The first three pairs of stitches are 4 × 3. The fourth pair is 4 × 2; the fifth pair, 4 × 1. The vertical stitch is three mesh tall.

Herringbone Gone Wrong (see Illus. 91). Take a 2 × 2 diagonal stitch downwards and to the right. Bring the needle up one mesh to the left in the same row. Take a 2 × 2 diagonal stitch upwards and to the right. Bring the needle up one mesh to the left in the same row. Repeat to the end of the row. End with an up stitch if possible. For the second row, turn your canvas upside down (180°). Begin one mesh above the last one you just went into. Continue as in the first row. Use your thumb to pull back the stitches in the previous row. You cannot work this stitch on traditional Mono canvas.

Tied Oblong Cross (see Illus. 90). Make a row of 2 × 1 *Oblong Crosses*. Tie down each stitch in the center with back stitches. To make a back stitch, work from right to left, going under two mesh forward and over one mesh backward.

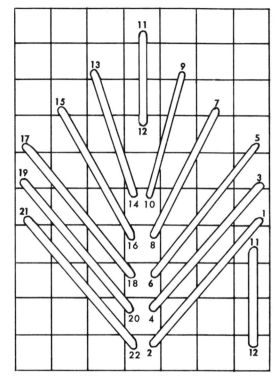

Illus. 89. Leaf stitch.

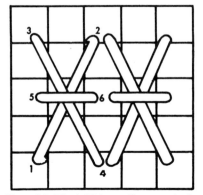

Illus. 90. Tied Oblong Cross stitch.

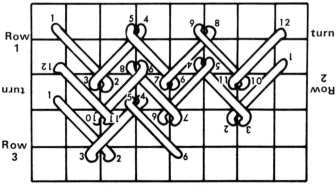

Illus. 91. Herringbone Gone Wrong.

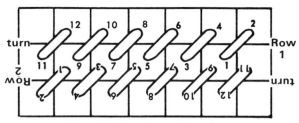

Illus. 92. Continental stitch.

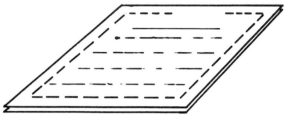

Illus. 93. Sew the pillow backing to the needle-point round three sides and all four corners by machine. Turn, stuff and sew the last side by hand.

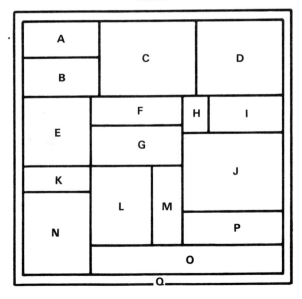

Work two rows of the *Continental stitch* round the outside of the squares of stitches. These rows add strength to the seam. Block face up.

Velvet, corduroy, or suede are ideal for the back of your pillow. Pre-shrink your fabric by washing it (if it is washable) or by having it pre-shrunk at the dry cleaners. Cut the fabric the same size as your needlepoint plus $\frac{5}{8}''$ on each side for seam allowances. Make cording, if you wish, and stitch it to the needlepoint so that the line of stitching falls between the *Continental stitches* and your design. Place the right side of the backing fabric against the right side of the needlepoint. Stitch three sides and all four corners on the sewing machine (see Illus. 93). Turn completely, paying particular attention to the corners. Make an inner pillow $\frac{1}{4}''$ larger on all sides than the needlepoint pillow cover. Stuff with 100 per cent polyester fibre. Insert this inner, stuffed pillow into the needlepoint cover and hand stitch the fourth side.

Illus. 94. Stitches used in the multi-stitch pillow:

A: Perspective	J: Diamond Eyelet
B: Double Straight Cross	K: Upright Cross
C: Herringbone Gone Wrong	L: Crossed Scotch
D: Patterned Scotch Crosses	M: Triple Leviathan
E: Plaited Gobelin	N: Double Cross
F: Double	O: Continental, Leaf,
G: Mosaic	Cross (initials)
H: Double Leviathan	P: Rice
I: Greek Cross	Q: Tied Oblong Cross

sections separated by Straight Gobelin stitch

Doll Pillow

A needlepoint doll, like the one on the front cover, will be a family heirloom for many generations to come. The crazy quilt skirt gives you a chance to make many different stitches.

Transfer your design onto Penelope 8 canvas as described on page 11. Illus. 95 shows the stitches that were used for this doll.

To achieve the alert expression in the eyes, work them in *Petit Point Cross stitch* (see Illus. 96).

Here, *Turkey Work* is worked three different ways to create three different looks. The doll's hair is worked with long loops that have been left uncut. To create depth of color in the hair, work each stitch with two plies of tapestry yarn in one shade of brown. Twist to those two plies one strand of Mohair yarn in another shade of brown. The center of the flower, also *Turkey Work*, is worked in a short, cut loop. A lace petticoat, created by making *only* three rows of uncut medium-length loops, peeks out the bottom of the skirt. If you use Persian yarn, the strands separate for a lacier look after being worked.

The *Upright Cross* (headband) is worked in two colors to give a polka-dot look. In the first row, skip every other stitch or dangle two needles threaded with both colors. Work the next row in all one color. Then work another two-color row.

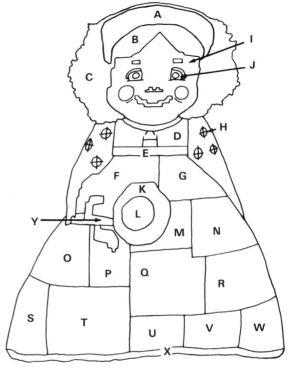

Illus. 95. Stitches used in doll shown on front cover:

A: Upright Cross	M: Star
B: Alternating Oblong Cross	N: Cross Diagonal
C: Turkey Work	O: Double Straight Cross
D: Fern	P: Crossed Scotch
E: Greek	Q: Brick Cross
F: Triple Leviathan	R: Rice
G: Double Star	S: Outlined Star
H: Wound Cross	T: Patterned Cross
I: Cross	U: Double
J: Petit Point Cross	V: Double Cross
K: Spaced Cross Double Tramé	W: Outlined Cross
L: Turkey Work	X: Turkey Work
	Y: Oblong Cross

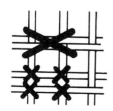

Illus. 96. Petit Point Cross stitch.

44

New stitches include:

Cross Diagonal stitch (see Illus. 97). Make a series of *Upright Crosses* which are 4 × 4. Place a diagonal *Outline stitch* between them.

Patterned Crosses Variation. This stitch is worked just like Illus. 85 except that you do not use any *Scotch stitches*. Replace them with *Smyrna Crosses*.

Outlined Crosses. Work a 2 × 2 *Cross stitch* and then place the *Outline stitch* round it. Vary the colors of the *Outline stitch* if you wish.

Wound Cross stitch (see Illus. 100). Lay a ground of *Cross stitches*. Then place the *Wound Cross stitch* on top of it. (This is *surface embroidery*.) Make a 4 × 4 *Upright Cross* which is actually four stitches (each over two mesh) that go into the center. Bring the needle from the wrong side of the canvas to the right as close to the center as you can get without actually coming up in the center. Then run the needle under the arms of the *Upright Cross* in a circular pattern. Do *not* penetrate the canvas. To end, simply stick the needle down into the canvas and secure the thread.

Brick Cross stitch (see Illus. 99). Work a diagonal row of *Upright Crosses* and alternate

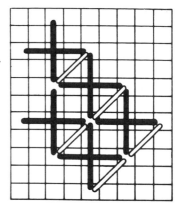

Illus. 97. Cross Diagonal stitch.

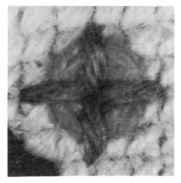

Illus. 98. Close-up of the Wound Cross stitch.

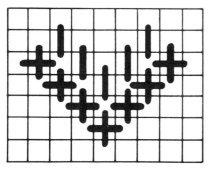

Illus. 99. Brick Cross stitch.

Illus. 100. Wound Cross stitch.

45

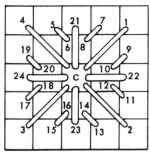

Illus. 101. Double Star stitch.

Illus. 102. Spaced Cross Double Tramé.

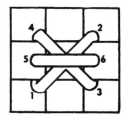

Illus. 103. Three Stitch Cross stitch.

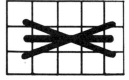

Illus. 104. Elongated Smyrna Cross stitch.

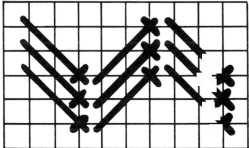

Illus. 105. Long and Short Oblique stitch.

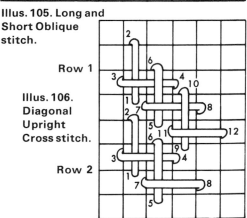

Illus. 106. Diagonal Upright Cross stitch.

with a diagonal row of vertical stitches that are 2 mesh high.

Double Star stitch (see Illus. 101). Make the X first. Then add the small stitches following the numbers in the diagram. Do the *Upright Cross* last.

Spaced Cross Double Tramé. Follow Illus. 102 to make this stitch, which is similar to the *Spaced Cross Tramé* in Illus. 57.

Place your initial on the bodice of the doll's dress; work it in metallic thread for emphasis. Then work two rows of the *Continental stitch* all the way round the doll. Block face up.

To make the pillow, cut a piece of sturdy backing fabric the same size and shape as the doll. Add a $\frac{5}{8}''$-seam allowance when you cut. To sew, place the right sides of the fabric and needlepoint together. Stitch on a machine with the needlepoint towards you. Leave a 5″ to 6″ opening, through which you turn and stuff the pillow. Trim the excess canvas so that it is even with the fabric seam allowance. Stuff the pillow with 100 per cent polyester fibre.

46

Painting

Reproduce an interesting painting in needle-point, and hang both copies side by side as a conversation piece. Illus. 73 is the painting and Illus. 74 is the needlepoint reproduction. For best results, choose a painting that has simple lines and little detail. Try to match the colors as best as possible.

Using tracing paper, trace the painting onto the paper. (Be careful not to damage the painting.) Go over the lines with a black felt-tip marker. Lay Penelope 8 canvas over the tracing paper and transfer the lines to the canvas as described on page 11. Paint the canvas with acrylic paints so that it resembles the painting. This also saves you from having to thicken yarn when the stitches do not quite cover the canvas. When the canvas does show through slightly, it is the same color as the yarn you are using and thus, not so noticeable.

See Illus. 107 for a chart of the stitches used to reproduce this painting. Note that the *Cross stitch* is used for the woman's entire figure, so that the stitches do not detract from the detail and shading. New stitches include:

Three Stitch Cross stitch (see Illus. 103). This is a 2 × 2 *Cross stitch* variation.

Long and Short Oblique stitch (see Illus. 105). Take a 3 × 3 diagonal stitch downwards and to the right. Complete a column of large 3 × 3 diagonal stitches. Then go back and cross each large diagonal with a 1 × 1 diagonal stitch upwards and to the left. The second column is the opposite of the first. Repeat the two columns to fill the area to be covered.

Elongated Smyrna Cross stitch (see Illus. 104). This resembles the *Smyrna Cross stitch*, but it covers a square 2 × 4.

Diagonal Upright Cross stitch (see Illus. 106). Each stitch is over three mesh and, therefore, is lopsided. Always cross it on the lower side of center. Follow the diagram carefully.

Notice in Illus. 107 that the facial features are done in crewel embroidery. Block face up.

For best results, take your piece to a professional framer and have him frame it. A good framer pulls your needlepoint across a stretcher, just as an artist stretches canvas.

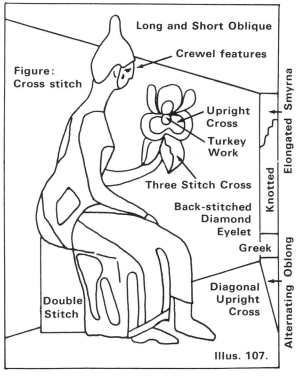

Long and Short Oblique

Crewel features

Figure:
Cross stitch

Upright
Cross

Turkey
Work

Three Stitch Cross

Back-stitched
Diamond
Eyelet

Greek

Diagonal
Upright
Cross

Double
Stitch

Elongated Smyrna

Knotted

Alternating Oblong

Illus. 107.

Index